winners' world

Biodun Olaitan

Winners' World
Copyright © 2011 Biodun Olaitan
ISBN: 978-1-907941-02-3
All rights reserved

''Extracts from the Authorized Version of the Bible (The King James Bible) , the rights in which are vested in the Crown, are reproduced by permission of the Crown's Patentee, Cambridge University Press.''

Email: nifepelumi@yahoo.co.uk
Phone: 07500048655

Printed in Great Britain

CONTENTS

DEDICATION

To all my mentors who taught me to keep
the focus

ACKNOWLEDGEMENTS

It is impossible for any author to deserve full credit for any work accomplished. To my dear family who were tremendously supportive and considerate throughout the whole process of writing this book. I would like to thank Adejoke, my beloved wife, and wonderful children, Nifemi and Pelumi for continuing to allow me the time to release my potential.

INTRODUCTION

I will like to see a winner as someone who has recorded success in their endeavours or recorded a string of successes. A winner may also be said to be one who loves to win at all times. The winner is also such that has an attitude to win always; here we will be see one who does not conceive failure but thinks of winning all the time.

It is interesting to know that you don't become a winner or a champion in the ring or period of battle or project till you have actually faced life challenges and won. It is then that you are declared a winner. So winning is an achievement that does not just come easily without a duel, sweat or struggle. In order to become a champion, you would have to look closely at the following:

- **Preparation** - This may include your planning and logistics. You will have to put everything in place so that you would have a smooth sailing in your project.
- **Training** - Here you may be required practice, rehearse or begin to sort out the modalities of your profession.

- **Habits** – This entails that you would have to put certain aspects of your life in check so that you would be able to achieve your goals in the course of your competitions or duels.

If you read the stories of great Olympic Champions, you will realize that they do not have to wait till the day of their competition to demonstrate their winning skills. An Olympic champion prepares ahead before the competition by training his or her muscles and acting as if the day has arrived. So such preparatory competitions are taken seriously and in some cases, they are made to compete against robots that may be better than them. Some athletes wake up early in the morning and run for miles in order to tone their muscles and prepare their minds for tough races. There have been situations where some runners have been pitted against animals that are able to run faster than them. Some Athletes are even put into psychological training so that they would be able to stretch themselves to higher heights.

It would be a disaster to choose to ignore or not give adequate attention to your opponent(s). Winners must have courage - not overconfidence. As a winner, you will notice that methods, strategies and planning differ from one athlete to another. This is because projects and opponents are never the same – so there is a differentiation of the skills and efforts needed for each competition.

Winners speak out who they are; they declare their intentions and are sometimes seen to be in the offensive. There would be the need to publicise your skills, profile and even create fear in the mind of your opponent. After all, the game is about who wins or succeeds in life. Having watched Muhammad Ali, one would see that he would have terrified and run down his opponent, not minding the size, stature or the strength of the opponent. Winners must have the warrior spirit to win - because the opponent has not come to laugh or dramatise in the ring or field of battle. Every contestant has a goal and aim to win; so they try to increase their winning stimulus so as to match up to each challenge.

Quotes

- I've missed more than 9000 shots in my career. I've lost almost 300 games. 26 times, I've been trusted to take the game winning shot and missed. I've failed over and over and over again in my life. And that is why I succeed. **Michael Jordan**

- ... Let me tell you what winning means? you're willing to go longer, work harder, and give more than anyone else. **Vince Lombardi**

- We know what happens to people who stay in the middle of the road. They get run over. **Aneurin Bevan**

- A champion is someone who gets up even when he can't. **Jack Dempsen**

- If someone is going down the wrong road, he doesn't need motivation to speed him up, he needs education to turn him around. **Jim Rohn**

CHAPTER ONE

THE IMPORTANCE OF PREPARATION FOR A WINNER

*'Proper preparation produces powerful performance' - **Tim Redmond***

The best way to succeed in any venture is to set proper preparation in motion. Thus in the scheme of things, every aspect of the project would be oiled. Folks have learnt to plan effectively and this includes painstakingly preparing before any project so as to achieve fruitful outcomes. You would know the quality of a project by the quality of preparation put into it.

Meticulous planning takes time and energy - that is why not too many people accomplish much out of their projects because they are not willing to commit their time and energy into what they are doing.

The wise and foolish builders
This was a building project in the Bible which involved two characters:
- The wise man
- The foolish man

It could be seen that it is not unlikely that they needed the same materials and setting. The reason why one failed and the order succeeded may be due to the fact that one planned, while the other had no plan in of any sort. See Matthew 7:24-27.

24   *Therefore whosoever heareth these sayings of mine, and doeth them, I will liken him unto a wise man, which built his house upon a rock:*
25   *And the rain descended, and the floods came, and the winds blew, and beat upon that*

house; and it fell not: for it was founded upon a rock.

26 And every one that heareth these sayings of mine, and doeth them not, shall be likened unto a foolish man, which built his house upon the sand:

27 And the rain descended, and the floods came, and the winds blew, and beat upon that house; and it fell: and great was the fall of it.

In the planning process, one would see that the wise man had knowledge about the setting for the building while the foolish man had no knowledge about the setting. As basic as that information may be, it was necessary to know what the outcome of building a house on a rock would be and the outcome of building a house on the sand would be. Sensible planning would have revealed to our foolish builder that his building site would not be able to sustain his beautiful house when it rains. So he would have needed the following:

- Research
- Soil testing

It is not unlikely that the wise man may have put a lot of issues into consideration before building his house on the rock. He would have found out the following:

- That the rock-site provided him a firm foundation.
- That there was not problem of erosion where he located his building.
- That no amount of adverse weather conditions would affect his building.
- That some others may have had solid buildings in the same location.
- The ways and means of attacking a project in the same vicinity.

Somebody once said that if you fail to plan, you will plan to fail. It is as simple as that.

Planning is an imperative factor that breeds success and this works over and over again. Whereas out Lord Jesus was looking at spiritual issues, this same parable is useful for everyday human activities. If you do not plan, you should not expect to reap great harvests or bountiful results.

Other planning perspectives
The Bible explores the idea of planning in Luke14:28-35 thus:

> 28   *For which of you, intending to build a tower, sitteth not down first, and counteth the cost, whether he have sufficient to finish it?*
> 29   *Lest haply, after he hath laid the foundation, and is not able to finish it, all that behold it begin to mock him,*
> 30   *Saying, This man began to build, and was not able to finish.*

31   Or what king, going to make war against another king, sitteth not down first, and consulteth whether he be able with ten thousand to meet him that cometh against him with twenty thousand?

32   Or else, while the other is yet a great way off, he sendeth an ambassage, and desireth conditions of peace.

33   So likewise, whosoever he be of you that forsaketh not all that he hath, he cannot be my disciple.

Do you consider building a Tower?
In the above parable, out Lord Jesus looked at a situation where anyone who intended to build a tower needed to do the following:

- He needs to sit down
- He needs to count the cost

- He needs to consider if he has sufficient resources to finish it. Resources here may be seen as the money needed to the project of the physical resources that would be needed for the project – like the lime, planks, iron sheets, metals for fortification, etc.

Now the fact remains that if there is no planning as outlined, it would proceed and lay the foundation and later be frustrated. Why? He started what he could not complete. The outcome is that he would attract mockery from neighbours and friends who will blame him for embarking on what he could not finish.

Ever heard of a Kind who wanted to make war against another king? What do you expect such a king to do? He would need to do the following:

- Take quality time to plan.

- Make consultations.
- Pull resources together.
- Number his population to see if he has able men who can fight the battle.
- He would need a good spy network.

Do not forget that the king that he is planning to meet in warfare has more resources than him. Failing to plan, he would sue for peace; the outcome of that may be a probable capture or loss of face.

The Planning mentality

Think about the planning mentality a serious mindset. This is the process of engaging your mind to the task and doing everything to begin to tackle the various areas that you would eventually encounter when the main event happens. We will take a close look at the boxing world. The heavyweight boxing champion begins to plan for a fight early. This may happen many weeks before the real fight.

You can train like a boxer (Information culled from: http://www.bodybuilding.com/fun/ss11.htm)

- Planning for the main fight makes you faster and stronger.
- To help you understand how to use the body.
- To help you understand how to stretch your body and maximise its benefits.
- To understand the art of throwing punches.
- To learn how to block punches.
- Knowing how to condition the body to absorb pain.
- How to survive the rounds.
- How to know the psyche of your opponent.
- To understand the actions and reactions of your opponent.
- Learn how to survive the rounds.
- Difficult roadwork to test and sustain endurance.

- Intense running that covers a particular distance – this helps to mimic the condition that the body faces in the round.

Let's look at a sample routine:

- Two mile run (moderate to fast pace)
- Sprint 100 meters
- Shadow box 1 round (3-minute round)
- Run backwards 200 meters
- Sprint 100 meters
- Shadow box 1 round (3-minute round)
- Sprint 100 meters
- Jog with hands up throwing punches 400 meters
- Shadow box 1 round (3-minute round)
- Sprint 100 meters
- Run backward 100 meters
- Jog 400 meters
- Walk to cool down

That is a lesson for us all to develop that planning mentality. Planning may take many weeks before the actual fight. Preparation is the only difference between winning and losing a fight. You'd be a looser to run a marathon without preparing yourself mentally and physically in advance. Notice that the preparation may be tedious and time consuming. All these are put in place so that success would be achieved. Successes are schedule events, preparation is tedious, laborious and time consuming. This is not actually a party or fun.

Other aspects of the training
Apart from taking regular exercises, most athletes eat healthily and follow a well organised diet. The period of training demands staying physically fit and sleeping properly. The various aspects of the preparation may be seen as physical and psychological which enables the athlete to develop a robust, covering more of mental preparation rather than the preparation of the body.

If a man fails to prepare adequately, failure will be the outcome. We see the same situation in the Christian perspective.

God the creator himself is a master planner that prepares ahead before any project. So winners should learn to follow His style. The following examples show that we should have no option, but to be prepared fully. That calls for a mental attitude that makes us feel that the planning and training process may be more important than the main event. That is the attitude that makes winners. It is actually true that excellence is more of a habit than an act. True.

CHAPTER TWO

DISCOVER YOUR UNIQUENESS AS A WINNER

In the previous chapter, we explored the imperativeness of planning and preparation. However, in order to get to that place where you can comprehend the essence of preparation, you have to understand how unique you are. This is because it is that comprehension of your uniqueness that will open the opportunities and doors of success.

What makes you unique?

That is the first question that comes to mind. This is a question that we must all learn to ask ourselves on a daily basis. This is a question that will enable us to be winners. You are who you are because of the things that you do. The things that make you unique may be seen thus:

- Your talents distinctly make you different from any other person on the face of the earth.
- Self-discipline will bring out the best in you and make the inner person in you shine out brightly.
- The self-confidence that you exude will also go a long way to help you build that image that will take you to great heights.
- The way you are able to manipulate your background will go a long way to determine how far you will go to be a winner.
- The vision that you have set out for yourself will make you that unique

person that cannot be easily duplicated.

- The drive locked in you will also define your uniqueness any day. So when others seem to take the back seat with all their loads of talents, you would be willing to shoot out with confidence and refuse to be intimidated.

How your background affects who you are Your background mostly determines your personality. So we are the products of our environments. However, we should not allow who we are to be looked down on. Folks tend to look down on us and seem to expect us to move and do things according to their own scripts that may have been written for them by their backgrounds. Do not accept such.

There is something unique in you because God looks at you and allowed you to be born in a particular location on the face of the earth. That is not an accident. It is for a unique purpose. So you need to begin to understand your uniqueness; that is how the best in you begins to come out. How are you able to make the best of your environment so that your uniqueness can be revealed?

- Maximization of all resources at your disposal.
- Learning to appreciate the gifts and talents that God has put in you.
- Learning to respect your environment and appreciating the fact that God put you in your environment for a purpose.
- Seeing the need for purpose and understanding how you can make things work.
- Learning to work with all the characters in your environment and seeing the best in them as you appreciate the best in you.

You can go on to achieve your goals

I know that I can because I am not intimidated by the problems that I see around me. I am not afraid of the load of uniqueness in me that inspires me to prepare vigorously. I am also able to take pain and endure hardship. Talent alone will not bring success; we need other elements that will help us reap the harvest of life. So how do I know that I can go on and achieve my goals?

- Firstly, I must believe the word of God that makes me know that bodily exercise profits me – but not in a massive way.
- If you can differentiate and separate yourself from the crowd, then you can begin to see a different picture that will propel you to greater heights.
- You must be a good communicator; one who is able to share his vision in a unique way. That is how you win. If you are not able to give voice to your purpose, then nobody will understand what you stand for. So effective

communication will give you an edge – push you ahead of your peers, other competitors and define your ideals and gifts.

Who lets the brand out? YOU

The brand that you create will go a long way to announce you and make you a winner. There are so many perspectives to you – so many that sometimes many folks die without accomplishing even half of what they have. The fact is that not too many folks know who they are. They have not even started to accept the unique gifts in them. They have not even begun to appreciate the gifts in them and they may not be willing to come to a place where they know that what they have is a winning brand. Why? They are busy chasing after shadows – they are busy living in the masks of others – they are busy looking down on who they are and what they have.

You do not expect others to announce you as a winner. It is you who will have to take off that mask – or those many masks that you are wearing now, and announce to the world who you really are. Then you will begin to take all the necessary steps to excel and be the true winner that you are.

There is something that you can do

As a winner, stick and concentrate your energy, strength and your mindset on things you can do excellently well than struggling to copy someone's gifting or ability. That makes you the original and brings out the best out of you in life.

Imitation Leads to Limitation

Be an original, rather than copy someone else success. God has some investment in each winner; discover that brilliance and uniqueness with God. Ideas are limitless if we can connect with God as our source.

Always remember that the value placed on original products is quite appreciated than another copy of those products. Have a deep thought, be creative, and make use of your mind effectively. Tap into God's creative ability for your uniqueness.

Never forget that in the whole world, there is no other being created like you that has same features, attitudes, character and DNA like you in the world. Work out and discover what makes you unique and special, why others should listen to you.

Why do you think your products or personality must be   given special attention from others?

Have you notice that there are things you enjoy doing (career, sport, business, and ministry) without struggling to do. Be passionate about the assignment, dream, talk and concentrate your strength on it. That is your uniqueness.

Every man is wired for a purpose from God. David Beckham is a gifted and talented footballer; he will never cross over to boxing. It will be a disaster of purpose when you envy somebody because of their success in one field and fail to discover and concentrate on your own uniqueness.

The fish will not struggle to swim in the water. You have been fixed and placed in a specific programme, agenda and environment by your creator. Discover your uniqueness and you will be on the list of winners.

CHAPTER THREE

THE IMPORTANCE OF IMPLIMENTATION FOR A WINNER

Have you ever reasoned out this simple Mathematics?

Thought + doing= RESULTS.

This is an important template that should guide our lives at all time. Unfortunately, many people do not progress to doing or the result stage. They may have thoughts – they may have dreams that they reflect on again and again, but they never proceed to that stage of using what they have thought about. So nothing gets done.

Think about the fact that if you do not take a practical step to do something, you will never get to the outcome stage where you would see results.

> James 2:14-24 KJV.
> *14 What does it profit, my brethren, if someone says he has faith but does not have works? Can faith save him? 15 If a brother or sister is naked and destitute of daily food, 16 and one of you says to them, "Depart in peace, be warmed and filled," but you do not give them the things which are needed for the body, what does*

You will realise that it is easy to have a thought and for many, it ends there. A mere thought. However, the day you deign to put your thought into practice, you are walking towards becoming a winner.

Winners think hard and put thoughts into practice. Every thought that remains untapped is like a dormant account that has no ability of yielding any financial gains. It is dormant, till someone makes an effort to reactivate it. Even then, that is a stage of DOING. It is only then that we would begin to see fruits or essential outcomes. Two basic characters come to mind – Abraham and Rahab. Their activities show that they moved from the level of thought to action. That is why they were able to see useful results. See James Chapter 2:

18 But someone will say, "You *have faith, and I have works." Show me your faith without your works, and I will show you my faith by my works.*

19 *You believe that there is one God. You do well. Even the demons believe—and tremble!*

20 *But do you want to know, O foolish man, that faith without works is dead? 21 Was not Abraham our father justified by works when he offered Isaac his son on the altar? 22 Do you see that faith was working together with his works, and by works faith was made perfect? 23 And the Scripture was fulfilled which says, "Abraham believed God, and it was accounted to him for righteousness." And he was called the friend of God.*

I have carefully observed all these years that no matter how you document a vision, if you do not take a complimentary step to implement it, you will never realise any fruit from it. So you should know that failure starts when winners refuse to take action in that great project they greatly believe in. Unfortunately, they never took action – their faith is dead – powerless – ineffective. So when next you go to the city and tell everyone that you have a great vision, you must have something to show in terms of the action that you have taken. You must show how you have put your vision or what you have thought about in practice. So the driving force for your thought or idea is your ability to put action in motion; or simply act.

There are many who are afraid to act because they are afraid of failure. These are a few reasons why you should not be afraid.

- You have not had the opportunity to test your thought, idea or vision.

- You even excel at the onset of your vision and be one of those great talents that would be admired.

- Your idea – even at the initial or middle stage can bring so much gain to you.

- Your ideas or dreams might be that one new invention that many are longing for – so if you are afraid of releasing it, you are short-changing yourself.

- There are a few people in the society that will hail you as a winner if you put your idea into action. Why? You may have saved their lives.

- The fact is that you should not expect all the stages of your project to be accepted by all. Why?
Different parts of ideas appeal to different people differently.

So I will be the first person to encourage you to put that idea in to action. Don't be afraid of failure or disappointment. Every winner or champion had at one time or the other failed in their area of discipline.
This is the right time for you to take action.

Begin today; and do not be added to the list of those who procrastinate; neither be like those who give excuses. Excuse is a friend to procrastination. Moreover, it will be encouraging for you to go ahead and do something so that someone would not steal your idea. Moreover, you should know that that same idea may fall in the hands of someone who may quickly do something about it.

Many years ago, I had an experience. I had an idea that I wanted to put into action. I wasted a lot of time and gave as many excuses as possible – saying that I would execute it soon. My 'soon' eventually dragged for such a long time that never came to pass. One day, I went out there and saw the same idea perfectly executed by someone else. I simply bit my finger; knowing that I would have been the initiator of that idea. Do not allow such to happen to you – so you can do all you can to move out and execute your idea today. I hope you will never find yourself in such a situation. However, if you do find yourself in such a situation, I must encourage you to pick yourself up and do something today with whatever new idea that God puts in your mind.

Do something today

- You can start that business today; do not wait till you have millions of pounds.
- Take advantage of the little resources that you have – a little can become a great deal. Like they say, little drops of water make a mighty ocean.
- Believe that you have what it takes.
- Start the football training or the marathon race.
- Start practicing that relay race so that you would not drop the baton on the actual day of the race.
- Go on and begin to write the first pages to that book you have always wanted to write – go on – do it.
- Start singing those songs you would like to record in your Music Album. If

you do not compel yourself to do it, you will never do it.

Most of my friends laugh when I tell them about the urgency of carrying out important tasks. The idea is that you do not have tomorrow. Today is your day – that is your day for action.   Don't delay because tomorrow is now. The acts of becoming a master is in practising the habit of doing what you love to do. Ask an Olympic champion, they will tell you they practice long before the competition. The same goes for anybody who has ever taken the wheel to become a driver, a pilot, a train driver, a machinist, etc. They have all had to start from somewhere – from a particular point where they had to practice – practice and practice.

It is in the process of practicing that perfection comes. You may think about it and not do it and you would not have the opportunity to perfect what you know. A baby that stays in the stomach for years will still be unborn, When that baby is born, he or she begins to do things.

The Driving Factor

It doesn't matter how much talent you have, how much money you have, how clever or lucky you are. The one thing that separates winners from all the rest is the following:

- The drive to overcome obstacles.
- The drive to realise their dreams.
- The drive to make life as fulfilling as possible.
- The drive to act on the best-laid plans.
- The drive to remain strong when the tough gets going.
- The drive to motivate yourself even when others are bent on discouraging you.
- The drive to excel beyond all odds.
- The drive to be creative and be prepared to use your creative instincts.

You want to be a winner? Then you must learn to take responsibility for yourself. You must begin to do a few things that will not put you in the class of the ordinary.

You must be willing to push yourself and refuse to give up and never be willing to be discouraged. You must be willing to do the following also:

- Push yourself towards self-fulfilment.
- Start now – tomorrow may be too late; or you may not have the same opportunity that you have today.
- Learn to know that you are the one in control – you are the captain of your ship; go ahead and sail away to your destined island.
- Do not allow your culture to mess your thinking. Even if you are at the mercy of your culture, you can still resist cultural idiosyncrasies and push through with your dream.

- Not even background, friends, family, spouses, neighbours can stop you.
- Do not be afraid of being successful; begin to tell yourself that you deserve it and you have earned the right to be successful.

What can stop you? Know this simple and important fact that the only person or factor that can stop you from being a winner is YOU.

CHAPTER FOUR

DEVELOPING THE RIGHT MINDSET AS A WINNER

According to The World English Dictionary, MINDSET may be

defined as the ideas and attitudes with which a person approaches a situation. So your mind set determines a lot in terms of how you approach a task.

- It determines how fast you can attack a problem.
- It determines the extent that you can go with a project.
- It shows the motivation that you would employ in the project.
- It will determine the length of time you will put in the project.

Note that you would ultimately be the architect of your success or failure. Your mindset determines that too. Also note that who you are is as a result of your thought. In other words, your thought determines the extent you will go in life.

Man cannot be greater than his thought. I will like to ask you this important question. What kind of thinker would you say you are? Would you say that you are an optimist or a pessimist? The idea is that not many of us know that camp that we generally belong to. However, the outcome of your actions would determine who you are. How?

- When you think positively, you will feel more in control, and you will believe that you will find a solution.
- When you think positively, you will be in the mood to achieve and reach your goals.
- When you think positively, you will have the interest to reach to great heights and no one can stop you. Without even realising it, you would mobilise all your senses and systems to bring about success.

The way you think strongly determines what kind of mindset you have. A winner must think right and positively. Your thought will shape your daily routine; it will shape your activities and relationship with people. A winner concludes in their mind before going for any event. A seed of victory must grow in you to bring out the attitude of a winner.

It has been proven right that when we repeatedly say a statement frequently and not give up, something good comes out of what we say. The fact is that you will get what you say. An action will invariably revolve round your statements or words. President Barak Obama's colour did not stop his ambition to be the first African - American President in the United States of America. He had a valid slogan that still guides many actions of people today: YES WE CAN. That's the right mindset that should permeate all our activities and actions. Against all odds or opposition, he stood his ground and maintained a positive mental attitude – winning an election that many did not expect him to win - not mindful of the environment or having a negative mental attitude.

The flipside of the coin would have been that Obama would have just come out to try his best or do all he can as many people would say. He would have retracted from the tough decision of going for the highest post in the land. He would have imagined that nobody in his shoes had tried and succeeded in his environment previously. With the mindset that Obama exhibited, many people who had wanted to try one project or the other would suddenly develop a positive mindset and say: YES WE CAN. Even at that, there will still be many who would do differently:

- They would sleep on their oars and firmly refuse to step an inch.
- They will rather enjoy the pity party or self discouragement.
- They would rather give many reasons why they cannot succeed.
- They would give as many excuses as possible – blaming the weather, the environment, friends, neighbours, etc.

Note that a positive mindset will take you to many heights and many great spots on the face of the earth. You just have to believe that you can do it; that you can reach the sky and make a positive statement for yourself and humanity.

Seeking for Opportunities

This world is a great and wonderful setting where many opportunities abound. You have the advantage as a unique resident on earth to tap from these bountiful opportunities that are free for all and sundry. It is interesting to note that winners and losers perceive the same opportunities each day. However, it is the way you specifically view these opportunities that will determine whether you can take advantage of them or not.

You may have heard of people who live on Gold mines without knowing the load of riches pilled underneath their dwelling place. They may still die in penury and want and keep wishing that one day someone would toss a gold coin at them without knowing that all the time, they were actually living on top of a Gold mine. One day, someone that knows what to do may just open up a mine there and show the residents the opportunities that had hitherto lain underneath their homes. They would scream, laugh, bite their fingers and wonder why they have failed to explore their environment or taken time to read through the historical past that would have given them a hint that God existed there.

The mindset of the looser will not be tuned to success or any atom of achievement. They would always be in the negative perspective – never hoping to win or assail. What would be running around their minds will be in the following frames:

- That they are complete failures.
- That they will never win.
- That they are nothing.

- That they are not capable of reaching their goals.
- That they do not have the strength to achieve or succeed.
- That the whole world is against them.
- That they are not able to control their minds and situations.

Having the mindset of a winner doesn't necessarily mean going around and telling everyone you are the best. A true winner believes that talents and gifts can be developed. That is why most winners would never relent in working so hard to actualise their dreams.

You can see success in advance before any competition or examination. As a winner, you will have a choice between failure and success. You will rather choose success and failure. You have a choice – you have an open road that leads to your dream – you have an open road that leads to that defined goal that you would not let go. All you need to do is to prime yourself to achieve your desired objectives. How?

- Keep your focus
- Have faith in God
- Be yourself – do not try to be someone else.
- Programme your mind to win; winners must have a preprogrammed mind to succeed
- Block your ears to criticism and all negative comments
- Learn to ride the storm of hardships, stress, hunger, and all challenging circumstances that will test your resolve to succeed

The mindset of the Ants and company
The Ants live in pragmatic communities. They are very hardworking and they are always ready to grab any opportunity as the go about looking for crumbs. There crumbs are stored for rainy days and adverse circumstances. In summer, you would see

them labouring so hard and you will see them all scattered about - busy. In winter, you will hardly see any ant around.

The focus and message is not the fact that they load up a lot to eat in time of adverse conditions; it is the mindset, the drive and effort that put into their labour that is enough to motivate the least of us. The Sluggard or lazy person is asked to take a trip to the Ant's shed in Proverbs
6:6-11.

6 Go to the ant, thou sluggard; consider her ways, and be wise: 7 Which having no guide, overseer,
or ruler,
8 Provideth her meat in the summer, and gathereth her food in the harvest. 9 How long wilt thou sleep, O sluggard? when wilt thou arise out of thy sleep? 10 Yet a little sleep, a

little slumber, a little folding of the hands to sleep:
11 So shall thy poverty come as one that travelleth, and thy want as an armed man.

The Bible gives some other perspectives of wonders which include the ants. Wisdom is an element of a positive mindset. You are either wise or foolish; you are either in the club of winners or in the club of losers – where do you belong. Explore the following and make up your mind.

24   There be four things which are little upon the earth, but they are exceeding wise:
25   The ants are a people not strong, yet they prepare their meat in the summer;
26   The conies are but a feeble folk, yet make they their houses in the
rocks;

27 The locusts have no king, yet go they forth all of them by bands; 28 The spider taketh hold with her hands, and is in kings' palaces. Proverbs 30:24-28

Looking at the characters mentioned in that passage, it will be exciting to see that inspite of the fact that they are not human, there is something about a positive and directed mindset in them all – apart from the enigmatic mystique that surrounds them, they are achievers of no mean repute. They are just destined for greatness; well defined winners in their own rights.

Can you change your Mind?
It is important to know that the mindset of the winner spells NO accurately. However, the mindset of the winner spells YES accurately also. Whereas you will see that that may be positive in the case of the winner, it is negative in the case of the

looser. That is exactly why they lose at all times.

Where do you belong? Simply changing your mindset will not come overnight. It's like learning to drive and after a bit of practice, everything clicks and it feels like second nature. Stick with it. You can change the way you think if you pay attention to it and adopt a positive mindset.

Three Gates of Control will lead us to know how to get things right.

The Three Gates of Control
The Eyes:
- The eyes that we have received from God are our tools for visualisation – that is what we do all the time.
- The power of vision has negative and positive effects on us – in terms of how our minds are controlled.
- Whatever your eyes dwells on for long period will form a picture or images on your mind.

- That picture or image formed will likely lead or guide your thoughts, which will later affect your actions. Visual images are hugely powerful. This is why TV adverts are more known as the best medium to catch the attention of viewers for any products.
- A picture speaks volumes in a man's heart. So winners must control and discipline what they see and watch.

The Ears:

- The ears are very important organs of the body. It is through the ears that you will hear all sorts of good things and bad things.
- It is through the ears that you can hear encouraging and discouraging words.
- Get that important gate disciplined so that you would not be led to abandon your great ideals in life. Stay strong and refuse to be discouraged. Whenever people around are

undermining your confidence, move away before you are discouraged.

- The ears are sensitive organs of the body that sometimes dictate some action we take. You will imagine that fear, intimidation, frustration, animosity, pride, etc, may all be reactions that may come about as a result of what we hear others say about us or about our situations. What you hear may go a long way to paralyse your spirit.

- Sounds play a significant role in the decisions you make in life. I will encourage you to choose what you hear or listen to; as well as carefully choose those whose words you pay attention to. They will either make or mar your life. Coaches sometimes employ psychologists to speak to their teams. This goes a long way to motivate the players and then plays a great role in their winning or losing the game. Whether winning or losing a game, the choice of words can make a lasting impact on performances.

- I will encourage you to draw support, strength and encouragement from supportive people. Team talks, motivational speeches and crowd support can be so powerful in helping you win a game. I dare say that you may be in a hostile ground and still train your ears to ignore the negative chants and vibes. The Bible talks of setting your mind as a flint.

The Mouth:

- I have heard many intelligent people say that the last critics you need to silence is the one inside your head.
- The little devil on your shoulder that keeps filling you with self doubt must be shut down.
- Fill yourself with words of encouragement always. Apply positive self-talk to help you negotiate through the terrible paths of life. Tell yourself, that you can do all things by

the special grace of God. Tell yourself that you can be happy – that you can reach the greatest heights in life. Nobody can help you sell your products, image and gifts than yourself. Maximize your self -talk.

- Do not forget that what you repeatedly say often has a capacity to stick and manifest in your actions.

Your mouth is your gateway to your success.

CHAPTER FIVE

LEARNING TO HANDLE PRESSURE AS WINNER

When you are hardly pressed by the project that you are engaged in, you will come to a situation where you feel that you cannot carry on. Your body may ache and all sorts of feelings and distressing conditions will confront you. But you have to remain strong and determined to achieve your goals.

Take a look at the different personalities around you and see how they are affected by pressure:

- The director of industry who suddenly loses his control just as he is about to complete the biggest deal or contract of his life.
- The boxer who unavoidably crashes before the final round.
- The talented student who messes up her final examination.

- The bridegroom who forgets his well-rehearsed speech.

Pressure can do funny things to us. If you're the one under pressure or at a disadvantage, you need to know how to manage that situation quickly. The common response to pressure is to retreat, go on the defensive. This is the reaction your opponents want to get from you so they can take over and sail ahead of you.

However, always counter the pressure with pressure. If possible change your tactics and methods but stick to your positive attitude to win. Pressure tends to make people act without thinking. If you can limit the time your opponents has to think and act, then you will benefit from their unnecessary mistakes.

Practice makes perfect
A person who has to get up in front of a big audience and do a speech might fret about it for weeks, lose sleep, sweat on stage and

stumble over words. But once they've done 100 such speeches, they won't be so nervous and so will have more control over the situation. The way we view a situation makes a big difference to how we perform, so by changing the way we think about a situation we can change the way we perform.

Controlling the pressure

Rather than thinking of how bad the situation is, direct your thoughts to searching for effective ways to improve the situation. Have a warrior mindset. Think right and correctly when under pressure. If you have to step outside your comfort zone, remember when things have gone well in the past, and use that experience to gear up yourself.

Positive self-talk can build up your courage instantly; and selfconfession of what you can do can also help you to activate your mind to achieve a great deal.

Always prepare and practice as much as you can. Focus on what you can control, not what you cannot. I have come to realise that your behaviour and attitude are two things you can always control if you want to. So how do you approach both of them so that they would not stand on your way to achieving success?

As one who anticipates being a winner, you must guard your heart with all diligence. This is the source of your victory. Your behaviour or attitude must be put in check. It will be suggested that you put a check on those negative traits that would try to leak out to soil or taint your progress.

If there is discipline in place, you will not fail to attain your goals. I have seen many people fail because they would not separate themselves from their stinking attitude. There must be a point of departure from attitudes that makes success unattainable.

Three factors that help to steady your nerves

Time factor

When we feel we don't have enough time to complete a project, we can panic. When you feel like you're acting without taking time, do a double take. People sometimes reports failure when they think too much or have too much time to think.

Priorities

- Do you really need to reply to that email now?
- Should you answer that phone call now?
- Do you have to write up the minutes of that meeting or could you delegate it?

Doing what we need to do and what we'd like to do are often two very different things. The number one rule in time management is prioritisation. That is arranging and organising your day in advance. Draw up a timetable, listing tasks in order of importance, and stick to this timetable. Do you know that; most emails can wait; most phone calls or text messages can be returned when it suits you, and most television programmes can be recorded to be watched later?

Winners know that in order to succeed they must avoid unnecessary corners such as poor time management. Don't be afraid to shut yourself off from the distractions of the outside world occasionally. If we maintain concentration and keep ourselves free from interruption, it's amazing how much we can accomplish in a short space of time.

The Competence factor
Negative thoughts are hugely influential, when we have a sudden crisis of confidence and begin to doubt ourselves, we will actually mess up. Your mindset must be positively tuned even when you face the mountain. Always try to mentally rehearse everything in your mind before any project. Believe that you can do it.

Once again, I remember Barak Obama during the campaign of the election in 2009, it was an unrealistic venture, taking the colour, and background of the man, but Obama stuck to his positive mindset and slogan; ''YES WE CAN'' and it worked. This was how he was able to win over many people as he cut across races, religions, peoples and age groups. The best way to avoid the worst is to focus on achieving your best by concentrating on what you can control.

CHAPTER SIX

EXPECTATION

'The atmosphere of expectancy is the breeding ground of Miracles.' **Rod Parsley**

I have lived a life of expectation and I have personally seen that those who have positive expectations cannot be put to shame. Expectation is like climbing a high ladder; you climb from one rung to another – hoping to conquer the point of your expectation. There are so many perspectives to expectations like the following:

- Expectation births manifestation; you have to have expectations in order to have outcomes.
- Note that as a winner you have to come to a point where you would be expecting your programmes to yield positive results.

- A woman pregnant with a baby needs no announcement; the result will be for everyone to see.
- The law of expectation reveals what you think has a powerful and undeniable impact on everyone you meet.
- Winners have a positive mindset about victory before setting on the course.
- Winners prepare the celebration party before the contest. That is what expectation is all about.

God wants men to be expectant as result of our faith in Him. Expectation increases your confidence in a competition, project, or marriage. Winners build their expectation based on information or misinformation from the past. They influence our attitudes, actions in the present and impact others in the future. We must be careful to set our expectation realistically and smartly. The audience, football fans, congregation, public, etc, are waiting either for entertainment, information or impartation from the winner, the man seeing all around him must be motivated to give his best performance during the encounter.

It was expectation that made Nelson Mandela not to give up the fight for freedom during the Apartheid regime in South Africa. Expectations boost our morale, increase our success rate and move us from one level of success to another. Take for example that you received a letter in the post saying you have won a million pounds or dollars. Before you tear the envelope open, you would definitely have an image of yourself thus:

- On vacation

- Driving a rolls-Royce

- Eating Caviar on toast

- Inspecting a private jet

- Owning a beach resort

Wait a minute, you suddenly open the envelope and discover that you have only been picked to win a million – the game had just started. You make a telephone call to the company and discover that it was not actually a real Lottery result – but a test ride. Your expectations die and you become deflated. Four things will likely happen to a winner in that mood.

- First stage is disappointment, you are disappointed that you failed, or did not win the competition.
- Secondly, discouragement.
- Third stage will be disillusionment.
- The forth and last stage is despair, an utter lack of hope. Here you have no hope that reality will ever meet expectation.

Winners should watch out for these four stages in their life journey:

- Disappointment

- Discouragement
- Disillusionment
- Despair

All these may occur during our expectations as we embark on certain projects, competition, etc.

Picture victory

I have always asked my close associates to keep their eyes on the picture; that object of their minds. It is such a beautiful thing to keep your eyes on that anticipated outcome manifested in a trophy.

That is the best way to picture victory. You cannot attain if you do not have certain anticipation. So the mindset of a winner must be fixed on the trophy or the medal. The more you anticipate it, the sooner you will get to it and achieve it,

There is no point waiting for the end of the tournament before you set your mind on the prize. That is the sort of lesson that we should teach our children. If you make it a habit to live a life of visualisation, you will discover that you will realistically not be far from the real victory. Generally, life should teach us that there is gain in anticipation – there is hope in waiting and a greater gain when you can visualize the object of your dreams.

It has once been proven that from age 0-6years are formative periods for children to develop good or bad habit as they grow. That is the age that we should ideally begin to teach our children to be great winners – teach them to visualise success and achieve and teach them to picture victory as if it already within their shores to grab.

In picturing victory, the following points must be closely taken into consideration:

- The mind of the winner must be set or focused on winning all times. If you lose focus, you will not reach the object of your dream and the trophy will be as elusive or as vague as ever.

- We must come to the point where we consider what we think about all day long. You must let your thoughts to be linked to that object of your dream.
- Since your thoughts shape your habits, and our habits always lead to actions, we should have clearly defined images that we feed our thoughts at all times. Do not give up, you will soon real the harvest.
- Never be distracted, discouraged or afraid of your opponent. You must have the confidence of the lion and the wisdom of the serpent.
- You must be able to look beyond the giants and be willing to walk as tall as them – if not taller. You are about to embark on a race and you are faced with all sorts of opponents. Your first instinct would be to be afraid of them. You might suddenly think that they are better than you. Whereas you do not have to underestimate them, do not overate them or be afraid of them.

- Fear will sink your hope of victory and you will never have the aptitude to achieve your maximum potential in the race. Look beyond the examination – look beyond the project – see victory in sight at all times. That will energise you and release a new vigour that will propel you to win the race.
- Hop over fear – what kills winners is not really the giants but the fear and dread of the giants.

Do you still want to be a winner? Do you still want to win the trophy, pass the examination and succeed with that project? Then you must picture the final outcome – that dream – that trophy – medal – that Certificate, etc. You are not going to let go of that prize in your mind's eyes for a second. Something positive will happen if you hold it close to your mind and you would soon find out that that image will soon become a reality.

Every form of distraction must be ignored; not even temporary distractions by other competitors. Do not forget that they also have eyes on the object of your dream. If they can, they would create a psychological upset that would distract you so you would shift your mind from your dream.

CHAPTER SEVEN

DETERMINATION

'A winner is someone who gets up to achieve even when he thinks he can't - Jack Dempsen

In life, determination will take you to great fields and you will reap great harvests. Many winners can be easily associated with that viable characteristic – determination. They would push with all their strength and keep pushing. Even when they seem tired, they will use the last effort to keep going until the conquer. The opposite is that those who are not determined easily give up and as a result fail to achieve anything.

Those who are determined seem to know the outcome before they achieve it. They always have a vision of their success and nothing would stop them from that visualisation. If you wake them up at odd times, it is likely that they will give you a vivid account of their task and how they hope to win. They will never be shrouded by fear or faces.

Show me a man or woman of determination, and I will show you great heights conquered in no time. Many folks have learnt this art and have always maintained a steady winning streak in diverse winning ways. Those who are determined have many characteristics:

- They never give up – they will run for three miles instead of two.
- They never flag in zeal.
- They are always ready to attempt harder tasks.
- They are always looking up.

- They never seem to get tired.

- They are hardly sunk by mistakes.

- They fall and rise soon after.

- They love ideas and they will always want to work things out.

- They take risks.

- They are very imaginative.

One movie that has actually inspired me is ROCKY I-IV. That is one source that has fired my determination in life. I have learnt how to be determined and how not to ever give up inspite any difficult situation that one may be passing through. One key factor on our route to winning is determination. No matter how driven you are, how great you follow your passion, your mission will finish at end line if determination is missing. Giving up is not a phrase commonly associated with winners. In other words, determination is a highly prized attribute of the winning factor.

Winners never think of failure, even though it happens. To a winner, failure is just an event which is not sufficient to dampen his or her enthusiasm. It may sound ironic that people who have experienced a lot of failure are in a better position to achieve success than people who haven't. When you fail several times and keep getting back up several times, you would stand a better chance to learn a lot of lesions that would help to inform your efforts in future. Moreover, you would be building strength, tenacity, experience and wisdom. As long as you don't give up you will never fail.

Warrior Spirit

The warrior spirit is a fighting spirit – a spirit that never says DIE. A spirit that will go to any positive extend to seek victory and excellence. True winners would develop a warrior attitude to every situation - fighting with their last blood. If you have to win, you must learn from the warrior spirit. Why?

- You will have a tough skin that can withstand all conditions.
- You will be poised to win.

- You will not have the attitude of a loser; you will be willing to go out and win at all times.
- You will not be afraid of the storm or adverse conditions – you will stay strong and willing to face any condition and win.
- You will not wait for the battle to come to your doorstep – you will go to the door step of the battle.

Developing a warrior spirit is important. That is one spirit that will guarantee victory at the end. You will not allow fear to be an inhibitor that dictates your decisions. A great weapon against fear is knowledge. Gather as much information as you can and consult experts in that line. I will encourage you to hit the ground running as a warrior. Being a warrior from the start or imbibing a warrior spirit will enable you to set the right agenda. Furthermore, being from the start will enable you to fight against your shortcomings and any obstacle that may stand on your way.

I have come to see through my observation of winners, that they are always warriors before victory or success. Your ability and strength in a particular project or event determines the output you get at the end. A warrior is tough, fierce, resilient and combatant. At the place of warfare, warriors are crucial fighters.

Fear of losing

No winner wants to trail behind. This mindset may not be as a result of egotism. It may be as a result of an inbuilt zeal or energy that is tuned to victory. If you see yourself as a prince, you will exhibit the characteristics of royalty. Another reason why winners are poised for victory is because they will not want to be seen as losers. Although many fail as a result of fear of failure. Some of us don't even make any attempt to succeed.

Some would not make much effort because of the fear of failure or may have the excuse that things might go wrong. Be prepared to shoot for the stars and the sky – that is your main target. But if you shoot with no aim, you are certainly going to miss your target. I have seen many people shoot and miss because they had not made up their minds to shoot in the first place. So there is the point where you make up your mind to shoot, visualise that you will hit the target and see the outcome even before you achieve it.

There are those who carry the authority of winners even before they approach the field of the contest. That uncommon anointing is God breathe. I believe that there is a place of asking God to empower one in a certain way in order to achieve in a unique way. Note also that the triumph gained in such a situation may not be for one to take glory. Most of the time it is for the winner to learn to give glory to God and use the victory as an opportunity to thank God, using the outcome as a means of helping others.

Coping with opposition and Persecution

Several things accompany victory and success. Victory brings fame, glory and popularity; victory brings glamour, material abundance and fulfilment. But all these achievements can't escape persecution, from probable opponents. Sooner or later, you will discover that success must be associated with persecution. Winners must develop a strong mindset to face all forms of opposition or persecution that will come against them. There will be situations when critics with negative opinions will strike with their venomous force – pulling down the walls of your achievements.

You cannot ignore the media, your family and friends and the pressure that they will assert over you on your way to success. Always remember that in every stroke of victory, there will be hidden images of persecution or opposition that would be manifested in the following ways:

- They will make your success to look cheap and easy to achieve.
- They will dig into your past, seeking for ways and means of pouring scorn on your parade.
- They will make it seem as if your victory was a fluke.
- They will do everything to make you feel bad about your success, so that you would not be able to enjoy your victory.

You will not give up, because the degree of success that you have will determine the degree of opposition and persecution that will be hurled at you by your enemies and so called friends. Most of their activities will be manifested as:

- Insults that have no basis or foundation

- Backbiting
- Misrepresentation of your success
- Uncalled for resentment or indignation
- Running down of efforts
- Victimisation of your person and the effort to make you feel that you can never win again

Persecution is a human factor that you must learn to handle and overcome. Your wisdom and fame will not save you from criticism; if anything, it will advance your course and make your victory sweeter. I will not personally see it as an affliction, but as a proof of promotion. But do not forget that affliction or persecution may be a trap of the enemy; but it will turn out to be a proof of promotion for you.

Persecutions are traps of the enemies to keep you from your goals and vision. They are meant to distract and weary you, so you may give up, from pursuing and fulfilling your vision. You must not allow them to deter your progress in the course of your journey. You will achieve success at the end if you do not give up or allow your detractors to stay on top of their game.

Welcome to winners world!